Junebat

Junebat

JOHN ELIZABETH STINTZI

ANANSI

Published in Canada in 2020 and the USA in 2020 by House of Anansi Press Inc.
houseofanansi.com

27 26 25 24 23   2 3 4 5 6

Library and Archives Canada Cataloguing in Publication

Title: Junebat / John Elizabeth Stintzi.
Names: Stintzi, John Elizabeth, author.
Description: Poems.
Identifiers: Canadiana (print) 20190172347 | Canadiana (ebook) 20199017255 |
ISBN 9781487007843 (softcover) | ISBN 9781487007867 (hardcover) | ISBN
9781487007850 (PDF)
Classification: LCC PS8637.T55 J86 2020 | DDC C811/.6—dc23

Cover design: Alysia Shewchuk

*House of Anansi Press is grateful for the privilege to work on and create from the
Traditional Territory of many Nations, including the Anishinabeg, the Wendat, and the
Haudenosaunee, as well as the Treaty Lands of the Mississaugas of the Credit.*

*We acknowledge for their financial support of our publishing program the Canada Council
for the Arts, the Ontario Arts Council, and the Government of Canada.*

Printed and bound in Canada

"Let be be finale of seem."

— WALLACE STEVENS

CONTENTS

Wing

ORIGA/ME

As summer inches onward and my life empties out
I apply for one more job, delete my OkCupid profile,
and begin folding butterflies out of coloured kami paper.
The asylum of the blank room, the idleness of sitting
on a borrowed chair at a plastic folding table
watching videos on YouTube of people I don't know
playing video games I'll never play. I'm sitting here,
headphoned and dead-faced, turning squares
into abstract insects and taping them to the walls.

The articulating fan shakes her head at me
but she cannot know how hard it is to be alive
sweating and losing every cent you never earned.
I learn another style of butterfly to fold, with rounder
wings, and watch the walls swarm out in colour
while on my computer the avatars of strangers
hijack cars in *Grand Theft Auto*. While a video
buffers, I delete Tinder for the third time this month
and realize I may be an isolated god.

I fold beasts into my unstable image — butterflies,
pigeons, bats — and remember the few weeks
in high school I spent folding even tinier cranes
out of the carefully cut corners of sticky notes
and ruled paper. The last crane was so small
I had to use tweezers, and once it was finished

I held it on the continent of my fingertip before class.
I stared at it, breathed, and the crane disappeared.
The big lesson I didn't learn that day was:
Breathing is bad for you — and I've paid for that one.

I'm not sure I can fold my life any smaller than this.

TO BE BESIDE ONESELF

Every time I catch my reflection lately,
I'm always standing beside me in it. I'm numb.

To be beside oneself, one is meant to be happy.

His hot breath fogs at my ear, his hand-hair
chafes against the back of my palms, my hate

sabres at knowing he is ever-nearby.

With him here, I want to lop the head off today
and gallop every stone night dead.

To be beside oneself, one is meant to be happy.

But I'm not, besides, I can't afford to see him
because I've been trying to imagine myself

within my own life. I am trying to personalize

myself to my melancholy, don't want to be neighbour
to my own narrative anymore. I'm losing sleep

eavesdropping on my traumas, over knowing neurons

have the capacity to ache, over knowing they're going
through something without letting me in it.

I feel as though my centre has unfolded, leant

over and spilled down the sewer drain of *him*.
I own his feet, his teeth, his cock. He owns mine.

To be beside oneself, one is meant to *be*

but as long as he's here, I am not. I am
trying to take my life personally but his skin

is vacuum-sucked into my bones.

He has stolen my bruises, my brothers,
each one of my busted hearts, and I'm trying

to forget his eyes, his shoulders,

and transcribe all that pain into me.
It is him I want to suicide, not me.

This skin — its visions as it loops

around him — are keeping *me* at bay.
I'm completely invisible in orbit of him,

a moon, light-shy, of inconsequential gravity.

And no one in this galaxy-cold city
ever holds the door for anyone but him.

SELECTED DEFINITIONS OF JUNEBAT

(*adjective*): of a noun which is neither a person, nor a place, nor an idea.

(*preposition*): continuing in time toward conclusion and stopping before reaching it.

(*pronoun*): used in reference to a person whose presence instigates an immediate, dehumanizing interrogation.

(*determiner*): used in place of determiners such as: *a/an, every, this, few, those, the,* or *many.*

(*conjunction*): used to conjoin two competing identities that are not real but, when joined, make up something that is.

(*verb*): to expect that someone will finally see you.

(*exclamation*): used to lament a closed door remaining closed.

(*adverb*): used only with verbs that represent a self-destructive action, such as: *deprecate, fear,* or *doubt.*

(*noun*): the creature you cannot admit to yourself that you are.

TOWARD HOBOKEN STATION (September 30, 2016)

Am I the station or am I the New Jersey Transit
train that hit it? Yesterday morning, the New
Jersey Transit station at Hoboken that sits above the
underground PATH train, where I'm heading to slip
under the Hudson to work. There's no telling which
one I am. I'm the one who stayed in bed, who woke
up to confusing text messages from a mother, but
I'm also the many wounded, every witness, and the
singular dead. I'm the track and the screech of late
brakes, the skunk-crossing sign on Ogden Avenue,
and the sound of rain rapping at my umbrella. It's a
symptom of psychosis, to be unable to discern the
part of the world which is you from the part of the
world which is invariably also you. That's why —
while I'm the photos of the rubble of the platform's
collapsed roof, the police tape keeping civilians back,
the fault and the passengers' fear creasing brows a
day away — I'm also the clouds, every droplet of
rain, and the too-many steps down this cliff into
Hoboken. I'm all that but I still don't believe I'm
the arms that hold this umbrella up. For a while
now I've felt at the whim of the locomotive limbs
of someone else's stranger. The drizzling streets are
no different today, no noisier or more quiet, and as
I go I feel less like the elbow and more the blinking
orange hand on the streetlight at Monroe, warning

bodies to either speed up to cross, or slow down to wait. The feet at the end of the legs people know me by kick along at a normal pace through the concrete Jersey. I fall in many bits, stream my way to rest in drains, puddles, and when I make it to Washington I stumble upon myself as a pot of mums in the rain, sitting on the curb outside the little grocer, white-headed and wrapped in purple foil. A few turns away from the station, the legs go on, not breaking stride, as I am every single hurt, wet thing on the Eastern Seaboard, as I am the heartbeat of New Jersey despite the fact I don't know anyone here, even though I am every stranger here except myself. On the last stretch and there it is, the station: crews at work, police standing outside. From this side of the building, there's nothing to see but the wariness, the blockade and a few New Jersey Transit trucks. Still, I am all tangled up in it — still a small, important clue trapped in the rubble of a body.

SALUTATIONS FROM THE STORM

Sometimes I wonder
if I'm really the best
person for this body.

Here, *sometimes* means
daily. *Body* means
cage. *Person* means

nothing at all, unless
you count this ghost, or
this storm. You can see

my haunt in the tired
eyes. In the limbs struck
like exploding oaks

as you assume you know
what this body holds —
which is never me

which may never be me.

I'd like to see my body
with someone else in it.
I just want to see it happy.

TO A SUB-HUDSON KINDCORE JERSEY PUNK

I have never written a love poem
for a man before but you
have blue hair and ride the PATH
between 33rd and Hoboken
and give up your seat to any lady
who gets on after you and you look
like you could roll out any punch
bobbing to the noise of your iPod Nano
with your dip-and-poke tattoos and you
have only looked me in the eyes
the once and that was minutes ago.
I've had a beer and am sitting here
while you've moved upstream in the car
where all I can see of you in the jungle
of Jersey-bound limbs are your pink
Converse shoes. I remember the first time
you and I ever shared a PATH car
a few weeks ago and it was so packed
a pregnant woman sat on the floor
in the corner near you and you said,
one earbud out, bending down to her
that you could kick someone out of a seat
for her. She said no but when a seat
opened up in front of me she was there
to ask me if I was going to take it
and I said no and I felt your gaze —

a bolt of lightning challenging me.
But just like this and we're off the train
now and I've lost your shadow
in the surge of so many bodies
climbing into the secret Garden State.
My shoes are the colour of your hair
only they're Clarks and I ought to put this
notebook away so I can pay attention
to the staircases but then I'm up them
and there you are in the distance
the sun setting down a bright
halo edge in your ocean hair.
You break stride down Washington
only to offer a cig and a smile
to a homeless man, and that smile
is becoming my nasty habit, isn't it?

THE JUNEBAT ON THE DUMP

The moon swallows the smog as it sets over Hoboken
behind Manhattan's jagged silhouette. At the base
of the cliff, where the body descends hundreds of steps
to walk to work, the sharp smell of garbage loiters.
The trash facility sits at the corner of Mountain and Hope
where discarded symbols go to be recycled into capital.
This is the place where imagination dies and thrives.
The Junebat is not here. The Junebat is a plastic bag moving
from street to street, searching for something to choke.
The stink of night has been foul a long time. Stink
of morning, stink of afternoon, too. The world stinks
with the dark image of a blurry, winged creature roving.
Some nights, the hardest thing to do is survive
in a world where you can neither find nor lose yourself.
There is no symbol in the dump to hold the Junebat down
precisely. There is no paperweight in the shape of their flesh.
The trash facilities of the world are quiet, as the Junebat is here
and not here, as the Junebat is both empty plastic and a body
trapped in wind and gravity and a sincere desire to die.
A breadcrumb-trail of garbage underlines Mountain and Hope.
Words fail because they were built to fail. A piece of sound
travels at the speed of a hydraulic press. There is no purifying:
the body in the bedroom of the night meets the moment
when it is ready to end, yet there is no ending-tool in reach.
They do not look out their window to see the plastic bag
of themselves flying sinusoidal. They do not smell the trash.

The window is closed. They are awake and alive and afraid.
Small words hold smaller meanings. Big words float on a huge
island in an ocean that won't end unless the world does.
The moon spits up the smog on the far side of the planet
as the sun decides to rise and forgive the sleepless.
The door in the bedroom is unlocked. Air lets itself in.
The Junebat is the body is the plastic bag is the wind
is the mountain is the dump of the mind is the hope.

WHAT IS A BODY IF NOT

What is a body if not   an empty backyard.

What is a body if not   the middle of a story.

What is a body if not   tomorrow, grinning.

What is a body if not   a cup of yogurt
                             expiring
                             in a thirty-year-old
                             fridge.

What is a body if not   a failed experiment.

What is a body if not   a forked road
                             without signage
                             overgrown
                             when you forgot
                             your machete at home.

What is a body?   Why have one?
                             Whose clay is to
                             blame for this
                             depression?

What is a body if not   a crumpled
                             paper flower

or a rhetorical question.   Don't tell me
                               the secret.

Don't tell me my body   is everything
                               or nothing.

What is a body if   I am inside of it?

What is a body if not   fire blamed
                               for its hunger.

It is essential   to have a body

just as it is essential   I remain
                               the ghost
                               astride it.

WAR WOUNDS

As soon as the idea strikes me, I'm lost: running
the shower hot, setting a can of Barbasol in reach
of the curtain, a fresh razor hungry in my hand.

My roommate is out and I'm here, stepping
naked into a warmer body, a steam coat
and an attempt at patience. There's no grace
to me. I lather up my left leg to the groin
by the fistful. The shower looks away as I prop
my leg on the lip of the tub and start hacking
leg hair like a machete tourist, following the grain.
My dad never did teach me how to shave.
I never really needed to. My first memory
of a razor was running my finger laterally
along one of his cheap Bics and opening up.
A little mouth, drooling in my muttering flesh.

It takes time. The water in the shower gets cold
and I switch legs despite knowing how much stubble
remains. It takes time to get things right; I shiver
with impatience, speed up, recklessly circumscraping
the knee, so by the time I've finished I'm chilly
and a little red river is snaking its way down
the front of my right calf. I turn off the water
and step back into my fogged-up life.

Learning things takes time. It's not easy
to shave a leg — it has landscapes unlike the jaw,
the Adam's apple, the upper lip. The knee juts, bends,
and if you end up nicking it the open cut will sting
only as it begins to silence. I dry off in my lonely kitchen,
feel my legs at once grip and slip along my baby-blue towel,
feel the hurt of my knee beginning to shut up.
My body is best at nothing but growing silent, so I listen
to the river as it mutes, as I walk through my apartment,
stopping only to dab at the red stream with a tissue.

Listening to the last whispers of my blood,
I sit down on my bed and marvel a little at the scars
that have returned now that my leg is bare. War wounds
from a rural youth, from bicycles and fake bravery.
From simpler times, on the outskirts of knowing,
on the outskirts of feeling like it could matter.
I rub my hands along my legs, now foreignly hairless,
feel the Braille stubs of the hair spelling out *failure*.
Tomorrow, I'll climb into the shower and spend the day
denying this gifted flesh, but I will come to conclude
that this wasn't meant to be, this played femininity.
That I'll follow neither my mother nor my dad.

But tonight, I'll marvel in this body a moment,
marvel in the feeling of the feminine elsewhere.
I'll lay the blood-dotted tissue open beside me on the bed
so I might study its Rorschach map to find a place

where I can lie down like this, every day, and feel old
and young and neutral and exquisitely baffling.

STILL LIFE, INTERROGATION ROOM

The door in the uneven frame is slouching.
Two nails have given up on a hinge.

The articulating fan can't find the words
to say why she can't see
what I'm asking her to see.

The hair on the neck of the dust unsettles.
Motes take up space where air should be.

Yellow rayon sheets, made in China, never washed,
huddle in the corner of a twin-sized bed
where the body often lies down to haunt itself.

A centipede's reputation is smeared on the wall.
A flock of paper butterflies and bats
and hearts is smeared on the wall with it.

Clutter on a folding plastic table made a desk.
Clutter on a hardwood floor bowing in.
Clutter on the sweaty, naked mind
crouched over a computer screen.

Shadows stain the corners of the room.
The light that breaks in from the window

and the room's one bare interrogator's bulb
doesn't add up to the shapes it casts.

The shadow of the body with paper wings
and a Mardi Gras of nooses.
The shadow of the body taking shapes
the body could never hope to have.

The body: shaved legs. The body: the shadow
of stolen lipstick. The body: remembering
the horror of its image in the one dress it owns.

The room's shadows dancing and dying,
refusing to be either still or alive.

The mind is where it always has been:
trying to make home in a white room
in an unsalvageable habitat.

It is the bell that moves to meet the clapper.
It is the body one must reshape
to make music with the station of the mind.

This is the sort of room
where a question can thrive
and suffocate in the same
measure of time.

Four walls can make a prison.
Four prisons can make a country.
Four countries a continent
and four continents a world
incomplete.

But the fingernails on the body
are baby blue and chipping
because some who wish to die
have not died yet.

For now, just forget the body.
Put your ear to this still life.
Listen to its silence ringing.

THIRTEEN WAYS OF LOOKING AT A JUNEBAT

I

Know this first: your mirror does not believe
in your wings, the only moving thing it will double
is a blinking fist — is a lurching eye
latched into a snowy mind disappointed.

II

A Junebat is simple
to drown or misdiagnose.
A vampire: ever in search
of a coffin to rest in.

III

Icicles filled the long window
like cocks fill a cellphone screen.
Look at them and ask yourself
if there's any way you want them
in, on, or around you.

Try to convince yourself
you're no Junebat after all.

IV

A man and a woman
are one.
A man and a woman and a Junebat
are one.

V

Upload a photo of the shadow
of your Junebat to Instagram
and filter it with Slumber.
Max out Structure. Max out Warmth.
Mute Saturation, tag yourself

to the back door of your home,
and delete every single
dating app from your phone.
Delete yourself. Delete
your phone.

VI

The Junebat is moving
so the Earth and the body
must be still. The Junebat
is singing so the Earth
and the body must be
gone.

VII

If you'd like to see me as a Junebat
call me *mister* or *sir* and you will
see me, crumpled paper bird,
in the flash of the rubble.
In my polite tolerance of you.

VIII

You know your bedroom, know
the creak of your office chair
and the gravity of it fighting
your drooping floor. You know
the stove, the carpet, the windows,
the dust. You know your eyelids,
your hand on a doorknob,
and everywhere you can hide.

But remember this:
the Junebat is involved
in what you know.

IX

Some days, I do not know
which to prefer:
the image of myself
in the mirror,

or the image of the mirror
in myself.

X

Don't not unforgive yourself.
Stack your negativity like laundry quarters.
Fold yourself into small contradictions, feed
on the Spanish warbling as you stuff
black and grey and white clothes
into frothy waterguts in Jersey City.
Take the advice of the women
when they tell you to dry on high heat.

Pull yourself to the edge of yourself;
look back swiftly and catch the paper wings —
wiggling from your scapulas — off guard.
When you get back home, continue
to hate yourself. Try to light
your wings on fire.

XI

You are not your body unless
you are. You are not your Twitter bio unless
you are. You are not a blackbird unless
you are. You are not a boy or a girl unless
you are. You are not your thirst unless

you are. You are not a symbol unless
you are. You are not alone.
You are not.

XII

The best way to look at a Junebat
is to look away. To shut your eyes
and let your screaming bounce them
back to you.

Junebats can only be seen
when your walls are down, when
the snowbanks grow tall as the skyline
and the world is frigid and flat.

This is where they fold.
This is where they fly.

The Junebats are at one
with the drifts. We too. We too.

XIII

It has been evening all afternoon
and yesterday for years.

The Junebat has been hanging
in the cedar-limbs
while it flits down the street.

The Junebat has always
and has never been before.
Between notness and ever
the Junebat flourishes:
an indecipherable clause.

HALE-BOPP

I found their ugly pink cactus head on the fringes
    of my commute through Hoboken last September:
spiny, beside another colourful sibling, and for sale.
    That was the time of my dying. That was the time
of an isolation so deep I could barely speak.
    The third time I walked by, I bought them,
carried them up those hundreds of steps
    into my life here, into my horror room.

        I named them Hale-Bopp, decided they were
            indefinite too. We lived together and I talked
        to them, and for the first time kin-words
            floated around in this apartment. We were
        similar, Hale-Bopp reflected *me* back,
            sat alongside my inferno, pricking me.
        I liked the tickle sent when numb skin hit them,
            how it could pull me back to the present.
        I felt close to a nearby thing for the first time
            in this city, and it was in their orbit that I
        didn't kill myself, didn't give in. Outsiders like us
            have a different gravity. We're on Jupiter
        while everyone else is on Mars.

Through fall, we were fragile sisters together.
    They sat in the room while I borrowed
their pink-headed bravery to write my novel,

until winter came and love started blooming
on Long Island. Weekends began to keep me
    away from Hale-Bopp and nearer to her. Winter
commenced with his yearly killings, but whenever
    I came back to Jersey I'd always go to them first,
in their little pot by the bed where I knew
    a warm square of sun would fall during the day.

    Hale-Bopp was my community, I their mother
        bird drooling water from my lips onto their dirt
    because I didn't own a watering can. I worried hard
        that they'd die over Christmas. Hale-Bopp
    was hardy but slowly they grew ragged,
        and the day after Valentine's Day I returned
    from a long stint in the relative bliss of elsewhere
        and found them crumpled in rot in the cold
    room, my space heater snoring from a bad
        breaker. Body brown mush, head gone white.

It's true, I didn't learn every cactus was a succulent
    until Hale-Bopp was already long dead, and it's true
I fumbled their pronouns in the same way
    I fumble my own in the privacy of my queerness.
There's much we didn't know about each other
    and yet all this hurt air we survived through.
Hale-Bopp was the symbol of the roughest arc
    of my life, and their leaving told me nothing
except that leaving was what I needed to do.

Poetry is the place where I go to be powerless.
    I didn't get rid of Hale-Bopp's body for days
after finding it. I lived with death in the room
        with me, felt the carbon dioxide they were
not trying to breathe, felt water pool my cheeks
        with no thirsty soil to spit in. My love lived
elsewhere now, in the girl out on Long Island.
    When I got rid of Hale-Bopp I wanted
to bury them but the ground was frozen.
    I had no shovel. Grief like that, quiet grief,
grief for plant-life, grief incomprehensible
        to others, can drive you to do rash, sad things.

Without a shovel, I found a stone in our tiny garden.
    I poured Hale-Bopp onto a spot there,
took up the stone, and beat them flat into lonely
        and gone soil.

        This is a place, but this place is no longer a place for me.

ANOTHER WEEPING JUNEBAT

After you finally come out and tell her
the shape you've found in your shadow
try and unpack why you shake and sob.

Are tears really your poison growing,
or are they the antidote to the dark?
The first spill once coagulation breaks?

She believes you. She knows you now.
She doesn't believe the dark blooms invading
your life are paper, but she knows they cut.

Maybe the tears come from imagination
meeting reality. Or reality meeting itself
to crack open your brittle, too bitter heart.

Or maybe the tears come simply from a fear
of dark, carnivorous flowers. Or that her
believing you makes this all so true

it could never not be.

Body

APOPHATIC JUNEBAT

A Junebat is not an analogy /
a ghost / an apology / a gender /
a joke / simple / a metaphor /
a fault line / synonymous / complicated /
a sexuality / a solitude / relative /
antonymous / a lack of gender / a question /
too much gender / natural / a shape /
a form / rhetorical / an approach to theology /
a held thing / a sensation / a holding thing /
mythological / fabrication / a careless thing /
a cluster / a careful thing / a word /
insensible / a state of being / a sound /
a reproach of theology / a hunch / inertia /
a body / an identity / theoretical /
a wound / forgiveness / a wound.

METAMORPHOSE

I.

Metamorphosis comes to some creatures
simple as *April*——heat and ache and silk—
—a stiff caterpillar digesting itself in the
husk of her own hiding——her heart's cells
split——her brain——split exponentially
into tiny unperson'd bits and reordered——
re-hardened——until a moth bugs out from a
breach in the gossamer——from a hole——
the escape-pressure pushing blood to her
wings——to teach her to do what she already
knows how to do

II.

There's no turning back from such changes————
when a *metamorphosis* comes as *realization* it breeds
regrets————certainty is the body digested————
splitting into tiny bits————and the resolve to
display this new being————to believe it————
is broken in conversion————doesn't add up in a
swamp of the brain where *subterfuge* is a quiet

    word screaming *PLEASE NO*————where the
complication in just breathing is distance————like
an inch of approaching between the hooks of
genomes————where there are no imaginal discs in
the pond————no decided way to emerge————
no instinctual fluttering————where every breach
is unwelcome and a horror but in many ways also
a   relief————a little show-off————painted
nails————rings————sentences overblowing like
"I'm your girl"————where you want everything to
be a moment of object-dissonance————the scrunch
of a brow————something to shake off————while
you also want nothing more than to just get caught

III.

A tadpole knows to quit using her gills when she becomes a
frog————————yet I don't even know whose lungs I've
got————————or really————————I *do* know————————I know
                                                                        exactly————————
but it's not clear why it takes so long for knowing to hit
you————————to hit *me*————————like sky light from a dead
star

————————and I wish for nothing but that the change
happens without effort————————that I'll wake up one day
liquid in a shell————————my cells reordering————————
pushing out the aperture of me into the wings of easy
pronouns————————but these changes are more in making
the paper of myself more origami-visible————————into a
Junebat who————————

    for all the wrong folds I've made————————looks like a
butterfly ————————blueprintless————————for the inhurt
I've endured not knowing what shape my frayed paper
wanted to be read as————————how hard it is to hold the
folds flat while they are setting————————how far away the
sky when you're exhausted on the ground————————from
  being alive————————and how difficult it is to try and fly

————————pumping your little wet wings————————
to prove you are correct————————while you're just trying
to hold yourself together

IV.

    It will take time for things to feel right—— — —for smoke
to clear from the mirror—— — —but it's speculated that
moths
    — — ——despite having been completely rebuilt— —— —
                still
have memories from their lives as caterpillars— —— —and
it is true when the moth's head emerges— ——— freshly
constructed
    from under the tarp cover of puberty— — ——it emerges
from the same spot where the hung caterpillar's head rested
    — —— ——when it had finished its spinneretting—— — —
      and such it is too—— —— —this insight—— —— —this
      re-evaluation of the soup of me in the body— ——— that
      after the silk scraps clear I am no different— —— ——that a
                        Junebat is basically
      John with an extra syllable —— ——where I'm still
myself *in* while trying to be more congruent *out*— —— —
where
    the coagulation of my split and resutured cells are as
confusing and inconceivable to be witnessed as they are to have as
                        bricks in me

V.

A Junebat is a sightless paper bat who has found a frozen pool to bounce
    their shouts against —— -
        to finally see themself bouncing in the air outside their body
                      so that the world
                    — -   yours —
           theirs
can see what messiness can exist in the mind's screeches in the body
    to finally see that it's actually a one-way flight — —— -
        — no U-turns — -
    where to discover you are a Junebat and to turn around would be
                            impossible
to have been as certain as to hear the paper wings flutter and still ignore
it would be to die - —
    would be to burst from the chrysalis of this being and into
        a Polyphemus moth –
      a moth who emerges from silk complete
                  beautiful and mouthless
                  living a short life— —
a moth who is named after a fearsome but easily duped cyclops
because of the visionless eye-spots on their hind-wings
      — - repulsing predators while starving to death
    a moth who lives such a short life but is still dazzled by streetlights

knocking against them over and over like a heart fading

for a Junebat is the kind of bat

that wakes up every morning

folds themself back

upside down - —- - -

until

after the days string on

everything starts to stick — -

and their visionless eye-spots

can suddenly see their world - ——

— - which is this world

in all its shapelessness.

CATAPHATIC JUNEBAT

A Junebat is an analogy /
a ghost / an apology / a gender /
a joke / simple / a metaphor /
a fault line / synonymous / complicated /
a sexuality / a solitude / relative /
antonymous / a lack of gender / a question /
too much gender / natural / a shape /
a form / rhetorical / an approach to theology /
a held thing / a sensation / a holding thing /
mythological / fabrication / a careless thing /
a cluster / a careful thing / a word /
insensible / a state of being / a sound /
a reproach of theology / a hunch / inertia /
a body / an identity / theoretical /
a wound / forgiveness / a wound.

Wing

THE NIGHT AFTER FLIGHTS OF CIDER

Tonight, and at the end of today, when
    we drove up from my place in Jersey
into the Hudson Valley and then back here,
    to your tiny studio in Hampton Bays,
I make every small adjustment to touch you
    as I lie beside you in your queen bed —
your feet, your leg, your arm. I'm a fencer
    bending into palpable hits,
I'm a heartbeat seeking home
    in her new bone cage.

We may not be in love, but I am,
    and tonight I'm gnawing at you,
eroding you like a pinch of sand
    in a long, tornadic breeze. Today,
the day after the night you painted my nails
    plum in Jersey, we drove up the valley
to see maple-dappled fall overflowing
    the hills. Storm King, Cornwall,
Poughkeepsie — and I pronounced it
    wrong the whole drive there.
"Plow-keepsee," "Poo-keepsee," until eventually
    you taught my tongue "Puh-kipsee."
I set its name tumbling out every hour
    breaking open the silences
to you, laughing at me, cracking our lulls.

You, separated but not quite single,
     are in no territory for me,
and I am not even exactly sure what I
     plum-fingered am.
This is not a good idea and yet here I am,
     the night after our day in the valley,
pressing at you in the night as if
     I'm simply spreading out in my sleep.
Today, we saw huge sculptures. We saw dogs.
     We walked a bridge across the Hudson —
halfway and back, actually, and you
     windswept-stared over the railing
that I bad-joked about throwing myself over,
     wondering if I could survive the swim to shore.
On the bridge we watched a tugboat push
     an empty barge beneath us. At least,
you watched the barge and I watched you.
     "Puh-kipsee," I whispered, your hair running
with the wind, and you laughed.

The maple leaves you handed me
     at the sculpture park
at Storm King were flattening
     in my notebook. There, we wandered
among girdered giants, across landscape
     expanses stretched between our marvelling
more at the turning leaves fencing
     the art in. We sat awhile in a swing

attached to a colossal Mark di Suvero,
    resting our feet and falling in love
with a huge elm tree. No seams
    held it together, no sweat or thought
forged it, no capital but sun
    and wet soil and time invested.
We dangled from man's accomplishment
    in astonishment of the elm
no visitor made this drive to see
    and whose influences no critic studied.
As others lingered near the swing, we moved on,
    and on our way back to the car you picked up
and handed me the deep red maple leaves
    and I pressed them between the pages
of my notebook as a souvenir.

I wonder if you are still awake, sensing
    the meander and ache of my toes
searching, sounding out for you
    under the sheets. My plum-tipped
fingers inch and reach as I reposition
    myself in the bed as a chance
for accidental grazing. My mind
    a race next to your repose, measuring
every instant of our day, this day
    and the days leading up to it,
of your hands shaking last night as you
    painted mine — such that for the first time

I can't see the flesh beneath them —
    measuring the intention of my being
invited to join you on a day-trip upstate
    because you said, "There is nobody else
I'd want to take." And I'm so afraid.
    The journal I've been keeping
has recently been obsessed with trying
    to convince me I am not in love
with you, that I am too messed up to be
    in love with someone who's too messed up
to be in love with me. I spin
    in the bed, trying to pin some piece
of the day down to prove my theories
    right.

We ended the trip with a stop at the cidery
    — Bad Seed — sipped flights and played
cornhole with a pair of locals, Tara & Dana.
    We won the first round and then over and
over they destroyed us. "We are not
    a good team," we said, before driving
south — exhausted — where never were
    two souls more relieved to see
the Long Island Expressway stretching
    darkly, traffic speckled and hideous.
"Puh-kipsee," I said, merging.

Despite my exhaustion — invited to sleep
    next to you in the queen bed instead
of on the tiny couch I've always deconstructed
    when you invite me here to escape the city
for a weekend — I am wide-eyed and hateful
    of myself. I hate how impossible it is for me
to not fall in love even when I'm actively trying
    not to, how the result of living
with little pressure between two things lets them grow
    too closely. Like weeds in the garden,
unwelcome, or like turning maple trees in the valley:
    nature is about getting close. I turn over,
look away, and let my butt sit against yours.
    Unlike the *Storm King Wall* —
a short cobble wall snaking around trees,
    slipping into and out of a creek —
I am unable to navigate the forest, unable
    to construct necessary space in nearness.
I stumble in and out. In my journal I sign off
    days as *Sara John*, or just *John*, or *Sara*,
write about isolation and possible suicide.
    I draw frightening self-portraits. Doodle
hearts next to the names. Discuss
    shaving my face and letting my face
stay unshaved. I swing. I talk to Sara, we list
    the reasons why you aren't to be loved,

how we're both far too vulnerable
        to be exposed to it. The fatal potential
of that kind of fall.

For months we have been exchanging emails,
        and the emails grew so long I decided
we should record ourselves talking
        and call them "Friendcasts." But the volume
of expression didn't decrease and the intimacy
        skyrocketed. It was in those megabytes
I told you, first soul, that I wasn't sure
        what exactly I was, did it by reading
to you a piece entitled "Elegy on a Boy."
        It was on a Friendcast that you recorded
an hour about how your husband's words
        hurt you, how anxiety was killing you, too.
I told you my thoughts — as a friend —
        "Fuck *him*." You left him only a month ago.

It is no use, this fatigue, this body. The bed
        is soft and I'm dense as di Suvero's girders.
The marigold trapped in resin and pewter,
        in the necklace I got you as a gift, sits
on the bedside table beside you. Your hair
        falls over the pillows in tributaries.
The clock strikes too late, strikes all lost,
        as the moon outside the window

sulks into the ocean beyond the dunes.
      I think of Storm King, think
of Zhang's *Three Legged Buddha*
      with a huge bronze foot pushing
a huge bronze head below ground, imagine
      that head and foot to be mine, think
of you watching that barge from the bridge.

I am lost and you are near me.
      I turn away from the window, back to you.
Softly, with my open plum-edged palms,
      I start to knead your sleeping back
like a cat. I am exhausted but I am not tired,
      so I know I can't stop.
"Puh-kipsee," I whisper.

GET LUCKY?

Days before Halloween and we're still wearing friend-masks
as we ghost along the Elizabeth A. Morton wildlife refuge.
We fall in step on the path between turkey-crowded trees
to the beach of Jessup's Neck, baystrangled between
the Noyack and the Little Peconic. At the nape
we stare hard and telescopic toward osprey nests,
spy on goldeneye trick-or-treating on the bay, try to
decipher the haunting of the salt marsh fog.
On the trails, off-season Hamptonites feed chickadee
and sparrow from their palms, as signs warn them
that this could lure rats. We didn't bring any seed,
we don't touch one another — no, not until an older
young man walks by us, toward the Neck, and asks,
"Get Lucky?" I smile, know he means *birds*, and say, "No."
You laugh and then loop your arm into mine
as we make our way to your van. Hours later,
life — as it had been — is finally sick of status quo,
and you lie down on your bed and I climb in next
to you. We gaze up at the blank ceiling, talking,
our molecules inching — for hours, it feels — until
they reach skin, until they swirl in fear of what
could come from two troubled rivers merging.
I turn your face to me. We float a moment in estuary.
Flaying our friend-masks, our costumes, we begin
to fashion a Frankensteinian sublime. It's nearly November

by the time we get lucky, by the time we unwind
ourselves free from this mummy-gauze.

EVIDENCE DISPROVING THE EXISTENCE OF A JUNEBAT

POINT:

Neither the chronologist nor the chiropterologist
    has heard of a Junebat.
    Therefore: there is no such thing.

FURTHERMORE:

Your mother and your father call you son.
    Your brothers call you brother.
    People on the street call you sir.
    You are nearly alone in thinking anything different.

You have written a whole novel from the voice of a
    character who could be called a Junebat.
    A novel is fiction; therefore you cannot be a
    Junebat, because it is fictional.

You don't correct the woman you just met at a book
    launch who has an extra black hair bow with her,
    and who's looking for someone wearing all black
    to give it to, and someone you just met gestures
    to you because you are wearing all black, and you
    gesture to yourself and smile, and the woman
    replies—laughing—"But he is a boy!"

You don't correct her because you believe she is
   right.
You are not a Junebat.

Sometimes you look at yourself in the mirror and do
   not hate your facial hair, or your flat chest, or
   your cock.

Also: don't even get me started on how you rarely
   even *think* about your cock:
   this is more conclusive evidence.

If you have a cock, you are your cock:
   Junebats (which do not exist) do not have cocks.
   Because cocks exist and Junebats do not.

You sometimes look at women on the PATH train
   and feel a desire to be loved by them, but also
   somewhat to be them?
   So what? Being someone else (who does not think
   of themselves as a Junebat) would not hurt
   you.

You feel deep sadness when someone at work comments
   that the notebook you have is pretty, then
   apologizes right away because she thinks you're
   going to be offended, but you say: "Thank
   you! I bought it because it was pretty!"

This has nothing to do with Junebats. You are simply
a depressed person.

In the visual journal you've started to keep, you write
things that insinuate a desire to die alongside
some exceedingly troubling drawings:
This is not Junebat-ness.
You are very sick.
Seek help.

While having sex you've never quite felt right has
nothing to do with Junebats.
Dissociation during sex is recommended.
Or maybe you are gay.
Gayness is real now.
Experiment.

You sign those journal entries with a compound name
crossing your name and a girl name.
You do this because you are trying to make your
depression exist outside your body (which you
know is male), and there is nowhere farther from
your body than the body of a female (in short:
you are not a Junebat).

Biology simply doesn't work that way.
Read a textbook.

Get a therapist (one that doesn't humour your Junebat talk like your current therapist does).

Assuming (for argument's sake) a Junebat is real, it's clear you aren't one because you're featured in a short documentary that someone does about what could be construed as an organization of Junebats, and when said documentary is shared on Instagram, the post talking about it is a series of clips of the people who are featured in the documentary and the caption says "click the link in our bio to see a short documentary featuring some members of our community."

You are not featured in the Instagram post, therefore you are not considered a part of their Junebat community, therefore: you are not a Junebat.

Remember how this post convinced you for a long time that you were not a Junebat?
Return to that frame of mind.
Build a house.

And that you have only recently begun to identify as a Junebat!
Impossible! It is impossible that you are only now coming to this conclusion. You are born and you are the way you are born. If you were a

Junebat, you would need to be a born Junebat. Otherwise: psychosis. Otherwise: too much time spent online. Go outside. Talk to someone in a bar. Go wander around Hoboken on a weekend night. Do you see Junebats? Do you? If Junebats exist you should see them. If you survive here, and (for the sake of argument) are a Junebat, why are there not more of you? There should be. It doesn't matter that you loosely called yourself a Junebat years before. It is a fad. I get it. We were all emo kids once. We grow out of things. You are online too much. Go outside. Use a public bathroom. Make a choice and stick with it. If you want to stand: there you go. If you want to sit: sit on the knife and go all in. It is really not that hard to understand. Blue and pink were picked for their difference. Adam and also Eve. It doesn't matter that one was made from the other. Not every Adam has some Eve inside. Go outside. Stop reading into everything so deeply. It's okay to not be a Junebat. That doesn't make you boring. Being a Junebat is worse than being boring, because it is not real. There is no such thing as a Junebat.

COUNTERPOINT:

I am still everything I think I am not

NEW WORLD BLACKBIRDS

Two blackbirds perch in the willow branches on the north side of the tracks of Stony Brook's Long Island Rail Road station. One hops directly into the air of the other's squawk, is sound-wound back to their former place a limb away.

The LIRR is a necessary segment of my leaving and returning to you. *Stony Brook, Huntington, Penn; Penn, Ronkonkoma.* Are we blackbirds too, I wonder, watching the gap and place names strumming out the hither-thither accordion of life. Mine: Long Island, New Jersey, all the liminal Oyster Bays and Pinelawns in between — Manhattan little other than a tall, pricey eyesore between your nest and my crowing post. Yours: a long and lonesome island. We hop in and out at each other, between weeks of off-peak LIRRs tumbling to platforms and making away with me. Branch split, we squawk — icterid we are — along the drooping wires of our separation — vacations from our simple ease as being us to interrogate and tidy ourselves. I put on my red wings as the LIRR incubates me west. You tug on your yellow head as you pull east from the station in your ex-husband's dying minivan.

You live on alone, calling lawyers, seeing your therapist, emailing your students and writing a novel you won't let me read. I go on alone, among millions of strangers, healthcare-less, student-less, too poor for therapists but brave enough to paint my nails and go off to secret Bushwick with my friend Lee to see queer bands and be interviewed for his short film on gender, where I'll joke that he should list my pronouns as "queer fraud." Your grandmother sends you Easter cards with your dead surname on it, I do my best to silently manipulate people into not describing me as a man. I ruffle, flutter up to stand on the tops of imaginary catkin in the Hudson, the sky backdropping me into a silhouette unnameable, while you're out thrushing yellow through the needles fallen from Hampton pine — digging for morsels. We sing out and I migrate east, on a commute of the heart. You stash your yellow head in the back of a drawer you may one day empty to make room for me and I slough my red patches and definition as we blur into a soft monochrome of us, a softness where I'm not pricked as I trip words from my head, as I try not to gender myself, and while I pretend — when I need to — my wings are true feathers and not these paper sinews, scribbled and dog-eared and too-many-times folded.

When I come back we rebuild that same messy, temporary nest, where we wear different names, break off the useful branches from our pasts, and hop toward one another, our jet beaks full with New World homemaking.

We plunge — plumaged — share in the solace and all
the while think how the squawking that birds make,
that these blackbirds make at this station while I wait
for the westbound train to arrive, could just be a game
— a way of teasing.

You were far before, so please go away again.
And then never — EVER — stop coming back to me.

RORSCHACH JUNEBAT

Blot #1:

whenever you see   me   you do not see
who I want you to see   whenever you see me
you   think you   know what   my contours   mean

wash your eyes   out with   Platonic shadows
focus on the lack around the blot   the card
stock   the contrast   place   the cave's   walls

Blot #2:

whenever you   you do not

see me   see me

so much as you see an invention of me

an interpretation   performing a   gentle killing blow

a breeze to a   lit wick   I'm not the forms

not the shadows   but the negative

space surrounding them   the weeping limestone

the smudged   edges of   the paper   the fold

where   the blot was   hinged on and   where

the ink is thickest   in hiding me   my body is not

the body   the shape   but simply   paper

simply   simply

corrugated   space

stone   without

want of   symmetry   without want   to mirror

my body is just   creased paper   it is you

who wants to   fling ink at it   my body is just

the wrapper that holds the   thing you wish to eat

Blot #3:

turn out the fire   tell the forms   to quit their march
    listen as the   cave and the page   blot to absence
  so thick you can feel it   tug the hair on your
                    neck
   lose your eyes and   listen   listen   for the screech
drawing the walls   sketching   the chains   on your arms
  mapping the path through   the system to approach
the sun   carry me there   and if you   make it
  notice how the clear   true fire   of me burns first
                the darkest
            parts of the page

AMERICA (I'M PUTTING MY QUEER SHOULDER TO THE WHEEL)

The night America took off her mask
we slept together poorly. I'd woken up early
that Tuesday, dragged myself to a gymnasium
in Jersey City to cast my vote into the void.
I came all the way out to Hampton Bays
to see her: her picking me up in that old
Mercury van, her bringing us back to her place.
As we watched the footage of the country
reveal its frightening hue, we were shocked
but not. A few days later I came back.

My nails were painted blue the week after
the mask fell from America's fist, the week
when the victorious hatred began. I walked
through Hoboken to work one morning
worried ten tiny splashes of colour on my body
might be enough to get me killed.
I realized then I had a choice: stay
queerly small and queerly quiet, or become
emboldened too. That like a true American Nazi
I could drop my mask and live life alive.

In the months after, I dismantled the mask
piece by piece while America lifted her skirt
to let free her pale hounds. I dipped my head

in cerulean dye and felt mortality pound
through every vein, felt myself climbing
to the paper surface of me. I let my body fold
and unfold. I let my body be loved by
a woman I loved more than air could explain.
I let myself be a foggy pile of indeterminate
me and I learned to love myself like that, too.
Despite the fear of the mortal danger
I grew bold in a way the system hated.
I decided that if this world was going
to kill me I'd die against the grain.
I decided that if America confronted me
with her rancid mouth screaming
I would stand as tall as her and scream back.

My nails, bright and tiny nodes of resistance
in the land of the craven, my hair, glowing
like a backlit sapphire in a home aflame,
I looked in the mirror and sang the words
of a new, loud anthem for this new, vast me.

IF YOU COULD SEE ME YOU WOULD SEE

If you could see me you would see

> a double-pane window
> with the inward pane
> broken.

> a softly curved face
> with brighter blue eyes.

> a sharp, cold wing
> on an old, wide bird
> diving into the bay.

If you could see me you would see

> a limbo
> of limbs.

> a crowd thinning out
> after a free performance
> at an amateur theatre.

> you would see someone at ease
> but because you cannot
> see me, I cannot
> ever be that.

Instead what you see is not me, is:

> jagged angles
> 5 o'clock shadow
> a brusque voice
> with the curves
> of a broom closet.

If you could actually see me

> you would see
> lipstick without hesitance.
> painted nails without fear.
> breasts on occasion.
> hair to my ribs.
> any shape at all.

You would see

> a question without need
> of an answer.
> a song without need
> of a tempo.
> a book without need
> of a spine.
> a symptom without need
> of a sickness.
> a pain beyond the reach
> of a nerve.
> shameless femininity.
> shameless masculinity too.

If you could see me you would see

the end of this dead-end road

prove the signage wrong.

You would see an end

thriving.

You would see

how there's always

a way out

of the body

who swallowed you.

SLOW GOSLING

Yesterday, when your husband tried to dodge his divorce
again — on his wicked end of this wicked world — we watched
the war on our Hampton shore escalate between the swan
and a family of geese. Yesterday morning after you rallied
from the bed where your anxiety was wringing your heart —
from the progress of your leaving having been deferred —
we went out and did a whole house of laundry, and when
we got back we found the swan popping his featherblank
collar along the bay's shore, stalking two Canada geese
and their half dozen goslings.

The standoff was hiss and low-tide, wide wings,
the swan lurching to redefine his territory. One goose
baited, played an easier target with a wounded wing
as the goslings waddled after the other, naively,
as forward the swan crawled, his untricked head coiled
flat near his ass, inching toward the tailing goslings.
Before the laundromat, when you were on the bed,
I lay beside you trying to make you laugh, felt the shudder
of your pulse as you tried to pause your brain. Later,
the swan closed the gap on the goslings and his cobra neck
struck, taking the slowest child up into beak, flinging.

That gosling — ungrounded into skytumble — stretched
out into a suspended moment, hung neverending

until her parents turned, opened their wings and leapt
heart-first, squawking to defend. We stopped breathing.
Our downstairs neighbour clapped his hands in vain
trying to break them up. It's a horror, the way people
are treated, attacked by creatures we think we can trust —
by definition, by nature — simply for existing nearby.
It's a horror how paperwork can shackle us, how
bureaucracy can circle us inside with our torment —
how inconvenient it always is, escaping pain. But life is home
to no easy leavings, one can't cut bad ties with a slice.
At the crowded laundromat, before the slow gosling
flew, we busily stuffed washers with the mingling
of our garments as children ran between folding-stations,
watched hypnotic cycles, tugged on humming mothers.

Eventually, the two geese would repel the swan
long enough for their goslings to get away, five tailing
close as the last hobbled after. Later, night came quiet,
blurring into the quotidian. This morning you called
your lawyer, as I sat on the couch, sore from shouldering
our huge hampers upstairs. Now, we're on the porch again.
The slow gosling hasn't shown up, but below us
the five others are back, pecking at remorseless earth.
Between us and the goslings burns the ominous promise
of the swan's return, irony by familiarity with trauma.
I'll lie to you for the rest of the day. I'll tell you
the missing gosling is resting somewhere, safe and alone,

as we watch the family scroll across our lives, as we watch
a swan-white egret — in the tall grass near the shore —
catch and eat a struggling lizard, then a rat.

ANECDOTE OF THE JUNEBAT

I placed the Junebat in New Jersey
and locked them up atop a cliff.
They made their ambiguous history
surround that echoing cliff.

The city and the world ignored them
as they slowly formed their concrete blurs.
All the while the Junebat remained
a crushed and folded port of lonely pain.

Doubt took dominion everywhere
yet the Junebat grew blue and soft
and certain. They became an open space
like nothing known in New Jersey.

ON THE MURDER OF JUNEBATS

If you're the kind of person who wants to kill
people like me, I won't use love to stop you.
It won't work. You love thy neighbour until
thy neighbour needs killing. You treat different
as different even though it's a fiction of angles.
Take my life, wear it like drag, and let your gun fall away.
Wring no throat. Wear my life and dance
like a fucking tornado on fire. Feel the weight
of the questions, the dry bloodshot eyes inside.
Wear my life and let me stand beside you, calling you
things you do not feel you are. *Sir, Ma'am, Bro, Girl.*

If you're the kind of person who wants to kill
people like me, come here and take my life.
Feel how hard it can be for how easy *I* have it:
for the whiteness of my skin, for how I do not need
to fuck someone who could kill me legally
just to eat and make rent, and for how I tolerate
so many misreadings and how those misreadings
make me less interesting game for your hunt.
I want to dunk your mind into these dark inches
so you may live a day in a cacophony of self-hate.

You might be surprised to recognize these feelings
so let's fit my life on yours like a gun barrel fits
between teeth.

Wear it, hand it back, then tell me I'm not real.

CARDINAL IN RAIN

I space out this morning, a break in dismantling
my room into boxes mid-week before my move
from Jersey, and see — framed in rain and my window —
a cardinal flit onto the back-fence, then fly off.

A lick of wet red light is what he is, two seconds
burning me into noticing as I wait, in underwear,
for my life to happen or for my body to take me
under the Hudson to work. A cardinal in rain
for its moment perched on the naked wood fence
in the backyard that — last fall — replaced a hedge
between the plots, flat wood sinking in like roots.
An attempt at timelessness replacing green and flux.

Cardinal in Rain could be the name of a painting
capturing the liminal moment between brief landing
and leaping off again, capturing what I know of this bird:
a blurry stop in Jersey, a reconsideration, and away.

My box of books is scheming with Saturday,
as my twin-sized bed begs me not to leave them behind.
The hinges of the door I once nailed straight are closed
and my window's moulding is an old frame in the Met
where a redness might make a home. Time goes.
In the same backyard last summer a robin was nesting
in the little cedar tree my writing desk looked out at.

I — naked enough in the Jersey swelter — took their company
into my silent life as I struggled to stay afloat and wrote.

One night, though, a gust brushed up the cliffs
from Hoboken and shook my wits from the tree.
I sat inside, unable to see anything in the window
but my own horrid reflection. When I went out
into the yard the next morning I feared I'd find
the robin's chicks dead on the ground.
I didn't. But the nest was gone from the tree's limbs
and a few days later the mother returned, searching.

It didn't take me long to decide this place wasn't home
or home material. Living here, in this moment
of my life, had been a cold shower — a draft
slinking up the creaky stairs to my bedroom
to throttle me. This whole city is surrender-hungry.
To survive you must bleed compromise,
you must sharpen yourself into *not being*
except insomuch as you are consumable. You must
be a dry cardinal, ever in flight, never pausing
to perch and remember where you'd wanted to go.

What I miss most in my life is open spaces,
fields, time to linger, so many animals it's pointless
to mark one flying through. I'm not built
to fly forever like a sky shark — I'm a Junebat
screeching out a light, letting their windows hang

as living paintings. The rain is steady, this room
is old and everlonesome. My wings are tired
and watershy; my ink is a quiet, irksome wind.

I don't know where I'm going, the only thing
I know is that it's not here. I'm not a cardinal,
not a waterfowl, not a bird of prey. I'm a different
darting thing, paper-thin and migratory,
and soon I'll lift my matter up and stuff it
into the back of an old minivan. Soon, I'll leave
this twin bed whimpering on the side of the street
for the garbage men to take or leave. I'll never
know. For now, I will get up, put on pants,
shoes, a jacket, and arm myself with an umbrella.
I will go — cardinalward — and tear through today.

City, world, look out through wood-clutched glass.
That's me. I've paused. And I'm passing now.

NOTES

The book's epigraph ("Let be be finale of seem") comes from line 7 of Wallace Stevens's poem "The Emperor of Ice-Cream."

The four poems "The Junebat on the Dump," "Thirteen Ways of Looking at a Junebat," "Another Weeping Junebat," and "Anecdote of the Junebat" play off (in varying degrees) Wallace Stevens's poems "The Man on the Dump," "Thirteen Ways of Looking at a Blackbird," "Another Weeping Woman," and "Anecdote of the Jar." In particular, "Thirteen Ways of Looking at a Junebat" lifts some lines directly from Stevens's poem (in parts III, IV, VIII, IX).

The poems "Apophatic Junebat" and "Cataphatic Junebat" play on theological forms of thinking that attempt to describe the nature of the Divine through either negative or affirmative terms. More precisely, apophatic theology attempts to describe through negation (declaring what the Divine *is not*), while cataphatic theology does so through affirmation (declaring what the Divine *is*).

The title of "America (I'm Putting My Queer Shoulder to the Wheel)" is a modification of the final line of Allen Ginsberg's poem "America," which reads: "America I'm putting my queer shoulder to the wheel."

Poems from this book have appeared (in earlier forms) in my chapbook *The Machete Tourist* (kfb, 2018), as well as the *Fiddlehead*, *PRISM International,* the *Malahat Review, EVENT,* the *Puritan,* and my RBC Bronwen Wallace Award–winning "Selections from Junebat," which was published on Apple Books by the Writers' Trust of Canada.

ACKNOWLEDGEMENTS

There are too many people to thank, but here are a few:

Thank you, Stevie Howell, for giving this book an immense amount of feedback at a time when it needed you. This book would not be this book without you.

Thank you, Kevin Connolly, for believing in this book so much and for helping it reach its final form. I am so proud of it, and am made prouder by our collaboration. A deep thank you to the rest of the team at House of Anansi for helping to bring this book into its beautiful life.

Thank you, Michael Melgaard, for helping me find the secret passageways in the industry that—eventually and circuitously—led to this book finding this wonderful home.

Thank you, Kirby, for introducing my work to so many through the publication of *The Machete Tourist*. I am positive that many who read this book will have bought it from you.

Thank you, A. Light Zachary, for supporting my work and letting me know that I'm real, and for informing people that I exist. There is no "yunebat" like you. Thank you to fellow writers (and friends) Brooke Kolcow, KD Williams, and Kim Fahner for being excellent readers of a variety of these poems along the way. Also, a special thank you to Daniel Sarah Karasik, who shared my poem "Evidence Disproving the Existence of a Junebat" to the largest crowd my words have ever reached at the #TakeBackTPL read-in protest. I am so humbled and wish I could have been there to take part (as much as I also wish we lived in a world where such protests were not necessary).

Thank you, Carolyn Smart and the Writers' Trust of Canada, for the affirming and career-changing support I received through the RBC Bronwen Wallace Award. I remain gobsmacked. Thank you as well to Leigh Nash for the notes that helped bring the winning poems into their strongest forms.

Thank you to all who have mentored me, given me feedback, read alongside me, or published my work in the past. If I were to attempt to list everyone here, I would surely miss some, but we both know who you are — thank you.

Gratitude to the innumerable friends and strangers who have supported me as a human being and Junebat, who have challenged me, corrected me, and taught me along the way. Many people have helped me become the writer and person I am today, including the work of many trans and non-binary writers who have no idea who I am. Thank you for paving the way.

The deepest thank you to my partner, Melanie. My love for you inspired so much of this book, and you helped give me a reason to survive and write it. Endless love to my parents, Marjorie and Mark, for the endless support throughout this life, which has afforded me so much time and energy to give to my work. Thank you to Grendel, too — my good-luck charm and the very best boy.

If you find yourself in these pages, I hope you love who you find. To be a Junebat is to be a beautiful and true and deeply, convolutedly human thing, and any and all are welcome in our colony. Let's unfold the night together.

JOHN ELIZABETH STINTZI is a non-binary poet and novelist who was raised on a cattle farm in northwestern Ontario. They are the winner of the 2019 RBC Bronwen Wallace Award for Emerging Writers and the *Malahat Review*'s 2019 Long Poem Prize, and their work can be found in the *Malahat Review, PRISM International, Kenyon Review Online,* and *Ploughshares*. They are the author of the novel *Vanishing Monuments* (Arsenal Pulp Press), as well as two previous chapbooks of poetry. They currently live and work in the United States.